Making Money Fast Thru Short-Links

Table of Content:

Introduction

URL shortening is a method on the World Wide Web in which a Uniform Resource Locator (URL) might be made considerably shorter and still direct to the required page. This is accomplished by utilizing divert which connects to the page that has a long URL. For instance, the URL "http://example.com/resources/subcategory/Username" can be abbreviated to "https://example.com/Foo", and the URL "http://example.com/about/index.html" can be abbreviated to "https://goo.gl/aO3Ssc". Frequently the divert area name is shorter than the first one. An amicable URL might be wanted for informing advances that farthest point the quantity of characters in a message (for instance SMS), for diminishing the measure of writing required if the pursuer is duplicating a URL from a print source, for making it simpler for a man to recall, or for the goal of a permalink. In November 2009, the abbreviated connections of the URL shortening administration bit.ly were gotten to 2.1 billion times.

Different employments of URL shortening are to "improve" a connection, track snaps, or mask the hidden address. In spite of the fact that camouflaging of the basic address might be wanted for a real business or individual reasons, it is available to abuse. Some URL shortening specialist co-ops have ended up on spam boycotts, as a result of the utilization of their divert benefits by locales endeavoring to sidestep those exceptionally same boycotts. A few sites avoid short, diverted URLs from being posted.

Short URLs regularly go around the expected utilization of best level space for showing the nation of the starting point; area enrollment in numerous nations requires verification of physical nearness inside that nation, in spite of the fact that a diverted URL has no such assurance.URL shortening might be used by spammers or for illegal web exercises. Subsequently, numerous have been expelled from online registries or close around web hosts or network access suppliers. As per Tonic Corporation, the registry for .to areas, it is "intense about keeping spaces spam free" and may expel URL shortening administrations from their registry if the administration is manhandled.

What's more, "u.nu" made the accompanying declaration after shutting tasks:

The final irritation that will be tolerated went ahead September 3, 2010, when the server was separated without seeing by our facilitating supplier in light of reports of various connects to youngster explicit entertainment destinations. The detachment of the server caused us difficult issues, and to be completely forthright, the level and nature of the man handle have turned out to be very discouraging.

Google's URL shorteners discourse bunch has as often as possible included messages from disappointed clients revealing that particular abbreviated URLs have been crippled after they were accounted for as spam. An investigation in May 2012 demonstrated that 61% of URL shorteners had closed down (614 of 1002).The most well-known reason referred to was mishandled by spammers.

The accommodation offered by URL shortening likewise presents potential issues, which have prompted feedback of the utilization of these administrations. Short URLs, for instance, will be liable to link rot if the shortening administration quits working; all URLs identified with the administration will wind up broken. It is honest to goodness worry that numerous current URL shortening administrations might not have a maintainable plan of action for the long haul. In late

2009, the Internet Archive began the "301 Works" ventures, together with twenty teaming up organizations (at first), and who are short URLs will be safeguarded by the undertaking. The URL shortening administration ur1.ca gives its whole database as a document download, so if its site quits working, different sites might have the capacity to give approaches to redress broken connects to URLs abbreviated with its administration. Circumvention could be that a site gave its own particular short-links as opposed to depending on an outsider shortening administration – yet this isn't normal.

Abbreviated web interfaces commonly utilize outside nation space names, and are along these lines under the ward of that country. Libya, for example, practiced its control over the .ly space in October 2010 to close down vb.ly to violate Libyan smut laws. Inability to foresee such issues with URL shorteners and interest in URL shortening organizations may mirror an absence of due ingenuity.

Locales, for example, Adf.ly utilize various promoting systems, including interstitial publicizing, to create income. This may deflect pursuers.

A short URL darkens the objective address and can be utilized to divert to a sudden site. Cases of this are rickrolling and diverting to stun locales, or to partner sites. The short URL can permit boycotted URLs to be gotten to, bypassing site hinders; this encourages redirection of a client to boycotted trick pages or pages containing malware or XSS assaults. Little URL tries to debilitate spam-related connections from diverting. Zone Alarm, be that as it may, has cautioned its clients: "Modest URL might9 be hazardous. This site has been known to disseminate spyware." Tiny URL countered this issue by offering an alternative to see a connection's goal before utilizing an abbreviated URL. This capacity is introduced on the program by means of the Tiny URL site and requires the utilization of treats A goal review may likewise be gotten by prefixing "see" to the Tiny URL; for instance, the goal of http://tinyurl.com/8kmfp is uncovered by entering http://preview.tinyurl.com/8kmfp. Other URL shortening administrations give a comparable goal show. Security experts propose that clients check a short URL's goal before getting to it following an example where the shortening administration cli.gs was endangered, uncovering a large number of clients to security vulnerabilities. There are a few web applications that can show the goal URL of an abbreviated URL.

Some URL shortening administrations channel their connections through terrible site screening administrations, for example, Google Safe Browsing. Numerous locales that acknowledge client submitted content square connections, in any case, to specific spaces keeping in mind the end goal to eliminate spam, and consequently, known URL redirection administrations are frequently themselves added to spam boycotts.

Another protection issue is that numerous administrations' abbreviated URL arrange is sufficiently little that it is powerless against animal power to seek. Numerous individuals utilize URL shorteners when they share connects to private substance, and in reality numerous web administrations like Google Maps have offered programmed age of abbreviated connections for driving headings that uncover individual data like places of residence and touchy goals like "facilities for particular infections (counting growth and mental sicknesses), compulsion treatment focuses, fetus removal suppliers, remedial and adolescent confinement offices, payday and auto title moneylenders, respectable men's clubs, and so on.

Short URLs, in spite of the fact that making it less demanding to get to what may some way or another is a long URL or client space on an ISP server, include an extra layer of multifaceted nature to the way toward recovering website pages. Each entrance requires more demands (no less than one more DNS query, however, it might be stored, and one more HTTP/HTTPS ask for), in this manner expanding idleness, the time taken to get to the page, and furthermore the danger of disappointment, since the shortening administration may wind up inaccessible. Another operational constraint of URL shortening administrations is that programs don't resend POST bodies when divert is experienced. This can be overwhelmed by making the administration an invert intermediary, or by expounding plans including treats and cushioned POST bodies, however, such methods introduce security and scaling challenges, and are hence not utilized on extranets or Internet-scale administrations.

A few sites make short connects to make sharing connections by means of texting less demanding, and to make it less expensive to send them through SMS. This should be possible on the web, at the site pages of a URL shortening administration; to do it in a cluster or on request may require the utilization of an API.

A couple of surely understood sites have set up their own URL shortening administrations for their own particular utilize – for instance, Twitter with t.co and Google with goo.gl.

In URL shortening, each long URL is related to a Unique Key, which is the part after its Top-level space. For instance, http://tinyurl.com/m3q2xt has a key of m3q2xt. Not all redirection is dealt with similarly; the redirection guideline sent to a program can contain in its header the HTTP status 301 (lasting sidetrack), 302, or 307 (transitory divert).

There are a few methods to actualize a URL shortening. Keys can be produced in Base 36, expecting 26 letters and 10 numbers. For this situation, each character in the arrangement will be 0, 1, 2 ..., 9, a, b, c, y, z. On the other hand, if capitalized and lowercase letters are separated, at that point each character can speak to a solitary digit inside various Base 36 (26 + 26 + 10). Keeping in mind the end goal to frame the key, a Hash capacity can be made, or an irregular Number Generator so the key arrangement isn't unsurprising. Or on the other hand, clients may propose their own particular keys. For instance,
http://example.com/product?ref=01652&type=shirt

can be abbreviated to http://tinyurl.com/exampleshirt.

Not all conventions are fit for being abbreviated starting at 2011, despite the fact that conventions, for example, HTTP, https, FTP, FTP, mailto, MMS, rtmp, rtmpt, ed2k, pop, IMAP, nntp, news, LDAP, gopher, direct and DNS are being tended to by such administrations as URL Shortened. Normally, information: and JavaScript: URLs are not upheld for security reasons. Some URL shortening administrations bolster the sending of mailto URLs, as the other option to address munging, to maintain a strategic distance from undesirable collect by web crawlers or on the other hand-bots. This may now and then be finished utilizing short, CAPTCHA-ensured URLs, yet this isn't normal. Creators of URL shorteners, for the most part, enroll space names with less prominent or elusive Top-level area so as to accomplish a short URL and an infectious name, regularly utilizing space hacks. This outcome in the enlistment of various URL shorteners with a bunch of various nations, leaving no connection between the nation where the area has been enrolled and the URL shortened itself or the abbreviated connections. Top-level area of nations, for example, Libya(.ly), Samoa (.ws), Mongolia (.mn), Malaysia (.my) and Liechtenstein (.li) have been utilized and in addition numerous others. Sometimes, the political or social parts of the nation responsible for the best level space may turn into an issue for clients and owners, [4] yet this isn't typically the case.

Tinyarro.ws and qoiob.com utilize Unicode characters to accomplish the most limited URLs conceivable since more consolidated URLs are conceivable with a given number of characters contrasted with those utilizing a standard Latin Alphabet Administrations may record inbound insights, which might be seen freely by others.

Numerous suppliers of abbreviated URLs guarantee that they will "never lapse" (there is dependably the suggested little print: inasmuch as we don't choose to cease this administration—there is no agreement to be ruptured by a free administration, paying little mind to "guarantees"— and stay in business).

A lasting URL isn't really something worth being thankful for. There are security suggestions, and out of date short URLs stay in the presence and might be coursed long after they stop to point to an important or even surviving goal. Some of the time a short URL is helpful just to give somebody over a phone discussion for an erratic access or document download, and never again required inside two or three minutes.

Some URL shorteners offer a period of restricted administration, which will terminate after a predefined period. Administrations accessible incorporate a standard, simple to-say word as the URL with a lifetime from 5 minutes up to 24 hours, making of a URL which will terminate on a predetermined date or after a predefined period, production of a fleeting URL of just 5 characters for composing into a cell phone limitation by the maker of the aggregate number of employment of the URL, and secret key assurance. A Microsoft Security Brief suggests the formation of fleeting URLs, yet for reasons expressly of security instead of accommodation.

An early reference, which portrays

...a framework, strategy and PC program item to provide connectivity to remotely found data in a system of remotely associated PCs. A uniform asset locator (URL) is enrolled with a server. A shorthand connection is related with the enrolled URL. The related shorthand connection and URL are signed in a registry database. At the point when a demand is gotten for a shorthand connection, the registry database is scanned for a related URL. In the event that the shorthand connection is observed to be related with a URL, the URL is gotten, generally, a blunder message is returned.

The patent was documented in September 2000; while the patent was issued in 2005, US patent applications are made open inside a year and a half of recording.

Another reference to URL shortening was in 2001. The principal striking URL shortening administration, TinyURL, was propelled in 2002. Its prevalence impacted the production of no less than 100 comparative sites, albeit most are just area choices. At first, Twitter naturally deciphered URLs longer than twenty-six characters utilizing TinyURL, despite the fact that it started utilizing bit.ly rather in 2009 and later built up its own URL shortening administration, t.co.

On 14 August 2009 Word press declared the wp.me URL shortened for utilizing when alluding to any WordPress.com blog entry. In November 2009, abbreviated connections on bit.ly were gotten to 2.1 billion times. Around that time, bit.ly and TinyURL were the most broadly utilized URL-shortening administrations.

One administration, tr.im, quit creating short URLs in 2009, accusing an absence of income-producing systems to take care of expenses and Twitter's default utilization of the bit.ly shortened, and addressing whether other shortening administrations could be gainful from URL shortening in the more extended term. It continued for a period, and after that shut.

The most limited conceivable long haul URLs were created by NanoURL from December 2009 until around 2011, related with the Top-level.to (Tonga) area, in the frame http://to./xxxx, where xxx speaks to a succession of irregular numbers and letters.

On 14 December 2009 reported an administration called Google URL Shortened at goo.gl, which initially was accessible for use through Google items, (for example, Google Toolbar and Feed Burner). What's more, augmentations for Google Chrome? On 21 December 2009, Google presented a YouTube URL Shortened, youtu.be. From September 2010 Google URL Shortened ended up accessible by means of an immediate interface. The goo.gl benefit gives investigation subtle elements and a QR code generator. On 30 March 2018 Google declared that it is "turning down help for goo.gl over the coming weeks and supplanting it with Firebase Dynamic

Links" (albeit existing goo.gl connections will keep on functioning)?

Numerous suppliers of abbreviated URLs assert that they will "never terminate" (there is dependably the inferred little print: insofar as we don't choose to suspend this administration—there is no agreement to be broken by a free administration, paying little mind to "guarantees"— and stay in business). A perpetual URL isn't really something worth being thankful for. There are security suggestions, and old short URLs stay in the presence and might be coursed long after they stop to point to an important or even surviving goal. Some of the time a short URL is valuable just to give somebody over a phone discussion for an irregular access or record download, and never again required inside two or three minutes.

Some URL shorteners offer a period constrained administration, which will lapse after a predetermined period. Administrations accessible incorporate a conventional, simple to-say word as the URL with a lifetime from 5 minutes up to 24 hours, formation of a URL which will terminate on a predetermined date or after a predefined period, production of a brief URL of just 5 characters for writing into a cell phone, limitation by the maker of the aggregate number of employment of the URL, and secret word insurance. A Microsoft Security Brief suggests the production of fleeting URLs, yet for reasons expressly of security instead of accommodation.

Link shorteners have been around for longer than most people realize. A popular example is a Tiny URL which was launched by web developer Kevin Gilbertson in January 2002 and still remains popular. Originally, link shorteners were primarily used to keep long URLs from becoming fragmented within email clients. This was due to text wrapping concerns with displays used at the time. However, today URL shorteners are particularly popular for social media applications. Short URLs are both aesthetically and functionally more beneficial for platforms such as Twitter, where long URLs hamper ease of reading.

There are quite a number of popular URL shorteners today such as bit.ly and Google's goo.gl. While these services offer plenty to today's marketers, a tool such as Pretty Links can offer much more power and flexibility – as we'll see later.

Advantages & Disadvantage of Short-Links

Advantages of Short-Links:

Maybe the fundamental advantage is that a short URL is less demanding for replicating into a gathering post, or into an email. Also when posting on Twitter where the publication is constrained to 140 characters for the whole post. Particularly in the event that you need a Twitter post to be passed along to others, you need the delivery to be as brief as conceivable to prepare for their starting words.

Be that as it may, are there different reasons why and for what reason not we have to utilize these administrations? Here are the favorable circumstances and hindrances to utilizing URL shortened administrations. Points of interest of utilizing Email Signature Rescue's own particular short URLs in your email signature Facebook connections will open effectively on mobiles.

The purpose behind this is on a portable, any URL beginning with 'http: //www.facebook.com' naturally opens in the Facebook application, instead of the web program on the gadget. So on the off chance that you don't utilize a short URL to connect to your Facebook page, and somebody opens your email and taps on your Facebook interface, they will be sent to the Newsfeed of the Facebook App rather than your Facebook interface. Skype snap to call, snap to talk and snap to include connections will work in unsupported email customers like Gmail.

While adding Skype connects to your email signature, for example, skype: username call, this component isn't upheld by all email customers, as Gmail. By utilizing a short connection, we guide clients to the program to start with, which deceives it into opening the Skype snap to call work.

Email Signature Analytics

Afterward, we will present more astute Email Signature Analytics. You will have the capacity to track snaps to the greater part of your connections in your email marks, including your flags and pictures. This will be extraordinary for input for what customers are tapping on and needing more data about in your email signature and doesn't constrain answering to just connects to your site.

Most online email programming like Gmail, Yahoo! Mail, Windows Live Mail, Outlook.com and Office 365 have character restricts the email signature length. By utilizing short URLs we can diminish the measure of code created and this can fundamentally build the data, social symbols and pictures you can incorporate into your email signature.

In the event that you feel so slanted, you can utilize shortening administrations, for example, these ones, to make custom URLs, known as vanity URLs, which are identified with your image name.

For instance, the New York Times utilizes "nyti.ms" in the articles they share via web-based networking media. When you tap on a connection that contains "nyti.ms," you know you'll be coordinated to the New York Times site.

Points of interest:

Abbreviated URLs can show up cleaner in the collection of email, as opposed to the long URL, which may break once you hit send. This is an awesome method to make a URL that is both short and vital and reusable.

URL shortened is likewise helpful in utilizing Twitter which permits just 140 characters for each tweet, hence giving you adequate space to quickly portray your site page.

Utilizing this administration implies that their connections can be reused. The administration would then be able to screen the activity that has utilized the connection and give measurements to you to utilize. You can mark your abbreviated connections so they may contain catchphrases to enable you to recall or your own image name to impart to others. A shortened can shroud a connection, on the off chance that you don't need anybody to see the first URL. It likewise conceals any unattractive connections.

On the off chance that you are exacting about which URL shortened administration to utilize, at that point you can pick one which will have the divert capacity. It implies that the shortener administration will go along page rank data to the objective page by utilizing 301 divert. Along these lines, you don't lose page positioning with web search tools.

Disadvantages:

Some email projects could signal your messages as spam

Since you utilize short URLs that divert to an unexpected site in comparison to the URL appears, some email customers recognize this and could check your messages as spam. Lamentably, a few spammers utilize short URLs to camouflage interfaces in messages. Much of the time this won't occur, yet it could. You might have the capacity to get around this issue by guaranteeing you are added to your beneficiary's protected sender records. We suggest you attempt it with the short URLs and in case you're getting hindered a great deal, turn them off.

SCAMMERS LOVE THEM

Connection shorteners give spammers an approach to camouflage their connections, attracting individuals to false sites loaded with newspaper news and significantly PC infections. Individuals have gotten onto this, and thus, some refer to abbreviated connections as warnings of spam.

THEY NO LONGER SAVE SPACE ON TWITTER

In September 2016, Twitter quit including recordings, pictures, and connections to the 140 character tweet restrain. Organizations that utilize interface shorteners just for effectively tweet their substance never again need to utilize them.

YOU CAN GET ANALYTICS ELSEWHERE

A few people battle that most online networking locales on which you'd regularly share dense connections sufficiently offer examination, making the information gave by shortening administrations superfluous. While you can unquestionably get some strong information straightforwardly from most interpersonal organizations, the Fat Guy attitude directs that more is constantly better. Joining the details from Twitter Analytics and Hub Spot gives you considerably more information to work with than simply Twitter alone. So this point misses the mark, however, it's not really off-base.

At last, it's dependent upon you to pick regardless of whether a URL shortener is appropriate for your business' showcasing plan. At Fat Guy Media, we incline toward utilizing Hub Spot as a result of how advantageous and easy to understand it is. Whatever your inclination, we trust this blog causes you settle on an educated choice.

- Shortened URLs can be controlled with the goal that you think you are going one place when you truly are being taken someplace less alluring. Regardless of whether the short address hasn't been controlled, URL shorteners create such an arbitrary gathering of characters that they don't provide you some insight as to your navigate goal.

- On numerous abbreviated URLs there is no content which makes a longing for any client to tap on it. Nobody knows where the connection prompts, so there is nothing to constrain anybody to tail it.
- If the shortening administration you utilized for any reasons chooses to close down, the greater part of your made abbreviated connections will never again work.
- Some administrations don't give divert and you lose SEO openings. In a few cases, web crawlers don't perceive divert.
- Since there are such huge numbers of phishing tricks online individuals doubt the abbreviated URLs now.

Quite a while back individual's utilized URL shortening administrations to get a more reasonable and most likely more noteworthy, site address on the grounds that the ones gave by free site facilitating administrations (Geocities, Xoom and so forth.) were too long and unwieldy. As of late, be that as it may, the URL shortening administrations have seen a kind of recovery due to the productive utilization of miniaturized scale blogging on locales, for example, Twitter.

I utilized the bit.ly administration to get an abbreviated URL of this page. Kindly investigate the connections beneath as I should reference them later in the post.

Genuine   URL:
www.webdevelopersnotes.com/blog/hindrances
shortening-URLs/
Abbreviated URL: bit.ly/e6dly1

Truly, diminishing the length of a web address may spare you on a couple of characters on Twitter where the post can't surpass 140 characters, however, for every other situation there are some extremely evident detriments of shortening a URL and it's best to maintain a strategic distance from it.

> Shorten the URL, lose your image: The real address of a page on your site begins with the space name. This fills in as a pointer as well as aides in building and advancing your image.

On the off chance that you abbreviate the URL, you'll miss out on these.

➢ Shortened URLs can be befuddling: Though the encompassing content might be of some assistance, the abbreviated URL offers no pointer to the pursuer. For instance, investigate the two URLs above. While one can without much of a stretch decide the substance of the page from the real web address, the abbreviated URL is only a jumble of characters. The site page URL isn't an irrelevant substance... it can fill in as a guide for the surfer.

➢ The abbreviated URL isn't anything but difficult to review: Since the abbreviated URL is littler long individuals expect that it might be less demanding to review than it's more drawn out partner. I don't believe that is valid. Once more, investigate the above URLs. Isn't the real URL more distinct and less demanding to recall?

➢ The benefit closes down: Unless a business is fiscally reasonable, it will crash and burn and bite the dust. It's happened to a great deal numerous online administrations; for instance, Geocities which was pulled around Yahoo some time back! So if the URL shortening administration you've been utilizing close down, all connections will move toward becoming non-practical.

➢ The URL shortening administration goes disconnected: Even the most well-known sites look down circumstances. The same can happen to the abbreviate URL benefit you are utilizing. What does that involve? All connections will seem dead!

➢ Shortened URLs are dangerous: according to an article on the rumored TechRepublic blog, abbreviated URLs can represent a hazard to safe perusing propensities. Additionally, URL shortening administrations confront a considerable measure of manhandling and hacking assaults.

Highest Paying URL Short-Links

❖ **Petty Link:**

Abbreviate URLs and gain cash with Petty Link which is a standout amongst other URL Shortening for winning cash on the web. The beginning is simple. You have to make a record, abbreviate your connection, and begin winning cash. Insignificant is a standout amongst other approaches to winning additional money. You get the opportunity to profit from home while overseeing and securing your connection. Utilizing the Petty Link apparatus, you can make short connections. What's ideal, you get paid. It's a totally free device.

You need to make a record, make a connection, and post it. For each visit, you win cash. The payout is as much as $12 per 1000 perspectives. Also, you can get 21% Referral Bonus. It has the Petty Link Referral Program. Elude companions and get 21% of their income forever.

Its included Administration Panel enables you to control the greater part of the highlights with a tick of a catch. It offers itemized details. You become acquainted with your gathering of people. It has a low least payout. You have to win just $5.00 before you are paid. Installment strategy is PayPal. Besides, Petty offers the most astounding rates.

Also, it has a devoted help group to enable you to out on the off chance that you have any inquiries or issues.

❖ Ouo.io:

Ouo.io is one of the quickest developing URL Shortener Service. Its lovely area name is useful in producing a greater number of snaps than other URL Shortener Services, thus you get a decent open door for winning more cash out of your abbreviated connection. Ouo.io accompanies a few propelled includes and customization alternatives.

With Ouo.io you can acquire up to $8 per 1000 perspectives. It likewise checks different perspectives from same IP or individual. With Ouo.io it turns out to be anything but difficult to win cash utilizing its URL Shortener Service. The base payout is $5. Your income is naturally credited to your PayPal or Payoneer account on first or fifteenth of the month.

❖ Link Shrink:

Link shrink URL Shortener Service gives you a chance to adapt joins that you go on the Internet. Link shrink comes as a standout amongst the most trusted URL Shortener Service. It gives a propelled announcing framework so you can without much of a stretch track the execution of your abbreviated connections. You can utilize Link shrink to abbreviate your long URL. With Link shrink, you can win somewhere in the range of $3 to $10 per 1000 perspectives.

Link shrink gives heaps of customization alternatives. For instance, you can change URL or have some custom message other than the standard thing "Skirt this Ad" message for expanding your connection snaps and perspectives on the promotion. Link shrink likewise offers a level $25 commission on your referrals. The base payout with Link shrink is $5. It pays you through PayPal, Payza, or Bitcoin.

❖ Shorte.st:

Shorte.st is another extremely prevalent and most trusted URL Shortening Company. Shorte.st comes as an easy to understand URL Shortener Service with numerous inventive alternatives for profiting by adapting the connections you share. Shorte.st gives you a chance to win from $5 to $15 per 1000 perspectives for advancing their abbreviated connections.

For WordPress Bloggers, Shorte.st brings its WordPress Plugin which will help you enormously to support your income. Shorte.st has a low least payout of $5.

The installment is credited naturally on the tenth of every month. The installment strategies incorporate PayPal, Payoneer, and Web Money. It likewise exhibits a referral acquiring opportunity wherein you can win 20% commission on referrals for a lifetime.

❖ **Adf.ly:**

Adf.ly is the most seasoned and a standout amongst the most trusted URL Shortener Service for profiting by contracting your connections. Adf.ly gives you a chance to acquire up to $5 per 1000 perspectives. In any case, the income relies on the socioeconomics of clients who go ahead to tap the abbreviated connection by Adf.ly.

It offers an extremely exhaustive revealing framework for following the execution of your every abbreviated URL. The base payout is kept low, and it is $5. It pays on the tenth of consistently. You can get your income through PayPal, Payza, or Alert Pay. Adf.ly additionally runs a referral program wherein you can win a level 20% commission for every referral for a lifetime.

How to Create Short-Links

When you begin adding UTM labels to URLs, they can get considerably more, and more mind-boggling. We require these labels to enable us to track the URLs, however, the more they are, the more improbable individuals are to recollect them. That is the place the URL shortener comes in to spare the day. They contract the number of characters in the URL to make it simpler to share the connection on the web, regardless of whether it's by means of email, web-based social networking, or downloadable PDF.

A few administrations give the capacity to track the connection snaps and keep a document of each URL you abbreviate, while others essentially give an abbreviated URL. Numerous web-based social networking planning stages and examination devices offer implicit URL shortening, too. Cushion will naturally utilize their URL shortener to abbreviate any connection you put in their framework.

In case you're searching for an administration to use to begin dealing with the length of your URLs somewhat better, here's a rundown of choices to look over.

As a matter of first importance, we might want to clarify about the Methods
Worked in Link Shortening:

This technique is the simplest, as the capacity is now incorporated into your WP establishment. It utilizes a similar URL that your duplicate of WP is introduced in, so this strategy improves joins with a shorter base URL, yet it functions admirably for any length. To get a short link for a post, basically, tap the "Get Short link" catch in the post editorial manager. You ought to get a fly up this way:

You would then be able to duplicate the short link in the case and spread it where you wish.
You can't a connection to outside destinations specifically with this strategy; however, you could simply compose a post connecting to another site to make a roundabout connection, particularly in WordPress subjects that help the "Connection" Post Format.

Jetpack by WordPress is a magnificent module from Automatic, the group that makes WordPress in any case. It coordinates huge numbers of the highlights of a WordPress.com blog specifically into a self-facilitated establishment, for example, examination, a contact frame, and a portable topic.

One component we're especially keen on is WP.me Short-links. When you empower it, it works pretty much a similar way that WP's worked in short-links work (see technique 1), yet utilizes the area http://wp.me rather, which is helpful on the off chance that you have a more extended site URL.

Re-coordinate Plugins:

This is a strategy I've utilized on my own site. It's somewhat of a workaround, yet it offers more control of your connections, without resorting to outside applications.

Utilizing a module like Quick Page/Post Redirect Plugin, you can make a blog entry which will naturally re-guide guests to another URL. It takes impressively more work than the initial two strategies; however, it likewise gives you supreme control over your short-links.

Furthermore, not at all like the strategy beneath, it should be possible without leaving the WordPress dashboard.

A decent technique in the event that you just need to make the periodic short link and you want an abnormal state of control over them.

Yourls:

This technique depends on a fantastic outer application, Yourls. There's a WordPress module enabling you to make short-links for your posts from inside WP, however, you will, in any case, need to change over to the **Yourls** dashboard for an organization or to make short-links to different sites.

The establishment is generally basic – on the off chance that you can introduce WordPress without anyone else; you shouldn't have any issues getting Yourls up and running. One admonition: It can't be introduced in a similar sub-registry (organizer) as WordPress or some other program since it needs its own .htaccess record. Simply make an envelope called "s" (for short) and introduce it in there.

Once introduced, you'll have the capacity to transform any URL you need into a shortlink, including every one of the posts and pages on your WP site. You'll have the capacity to pick the watchword in the short link or have an irregular word created (ala Bit.ly).

The dashboard likewise gives some great movement examination, which is helpful for understanding where your short-links are best.

Instructions to Make a URL of a PDF File:

Web software engineers utilize URL while making hyperlinks that interface with different pages and records. The URL (Uniform Resource Locator) tells your program where it can discover the record indicated by the connection. Most connections on website pages point to other site pages or picture documents. Be that as it may, an ever-increasing number of sites contain connections to PDF archives. Making a URL for a PDF record is like making URLs for other document writes. With a specific end goal to see the PDF record in the wake of tapping on the connection, the client should have Adobe Reader introduced on their PC.

Stage 1

> Open the program you use to alter your site pages and go to the site page where you wish to embed the connection to the PDF archive.

Stage 2

> Embed the accompanying HTML code: "Snap here to see PDF record" (without the first and last quotes.) The words "Snap here to see PDF document" will show up on your page as a hyperlink and will be the words the client taps

on to go to the PDF report. You can supplant them with different expressions of your picking.

Stage 3

> Supplant "URL" with the genuine URL of the PDF report. On the off chance that the PDF record is spared as "myfile.pdf" in an indistinguishable envelope from your website page, the URL will be "myfile.pdf". On the off chance that the PDF record is spared in a subfolder called "Reports," the URL will be "Archives/myfile.pdf". In the event that the PDF record is on another site in an organizer called "Reports", the URL will be "http://www.mywebsite.com/Documents/my file.pdf" (utilize the genuine name of the site.)

URL SHORTENERS TO CHOOSE FROM

* 7. Ly: A simple to utilize URL shortener that gives click measurements.
* 2. ADF.ly: This is a URL shortener benefit that pays their clients for utilizing it. You procure cash for each individual who visits your connection. http://adf.ly/ropye

- Al.ly: Another URL shortener that pays you in view of the number of snaps on your connections.
- Bc.vc: Shorten your URLs and acquire cash on your snaps. Agree to accept a record to begin winning from your mutual connections.
- Bit.do: A straightforward URL shortener that enables you to abbreviate, redo, and track your connections.
- Bit.ly: Shorten your connections and track the snaps on them. Illustration: bit.ly/c92v5e6
- Bitly.com: Another URL used to get to the Bit.ly shortener.
- T.co: Twitter's URL shortener – must be utilized on the social network. Example: https://t.co/Lwdslj087
- Lnkd.in: LinkedIn's URL shortener – must be utilized on LinkedIn. Illustration:
- Cur.lv: The URL shortener by CoinURL.com – a bitcoin-based promoting URL shortener choice to adapt your substance with bitcoin. Including a + image will enable you to see details of the connection.
- TinyURL.com: A well-known URL shortener that can produce its own shorter URL yet, in addition, gives you the choice to make a

custom pseudonym. The URLs won't break in email or lapse.

- Ow.ly: A well-known URL shortening administration that gives you a chance to abbreviate joins, share documents, and track visits.
- Ity.im: Another URL shortener that pays you in view of the number of snaps on your connections.
- Q.gs: Another URL to get to the Adf.ly shortener.
- Is.gd: Shorten joins with arbitrary or modified URL.
- Po.st: Social sharing stage that incorporates a URL shortener.
- U.bb: Another URL to get to the Adf.ly shortener.
- Qr.net: QR code maker from your standard URL.
- S.id: A simple to utilize URL shortener.
- Ph. Dog: Basic URL shortener.
- Tny.im: A straightforward URL shortening device
- Goo.gl: Google URL shortener. Case: http://goo.gl/sjpos4t
- Tr.im: Link shortener with the capacity to make custom catchphrase short connects to

help drive commitment and enhance active visitor clicking percentage.

- X.co: A URL shortening and URL redirection benefit from Go Daddy. You should have a record to utilize this administration.
- V.gd: Shorten joins with irregular or tweaked URL.
- Cutt.us: Basic URL shortener additionally incorporates a multi-URL shortener device.
- J.mp: Another URL used to get to the Bit.ly shortener.
- U.to: Shorten any connection. You'll have to make a record and login to see the measurements identified with the number of snaps.
- YOURLS.org: This is a free open source content that enables you to run your own URL shortening administration so you can control the area. Run your own TinyURL or Bit.ly, and incorporate details.
- PrettyLinkPro.com: This is a paid administration that enables you to shroud partner interfaces and abbreviates URLs. Evaluating keeps running from $47/year to $197/year relying upon the number of destinations you need to utilize it on.

- Filoops.info: This site offers a URL shortener, a URL tracker, space WHOIS query, and a Google Ad Stripper from AdSense joins.
- Db.tt: The URL shortener Dropbox employments. Illustration:
- doiop.com: An essential URL shortener that enables you to pick either an arbitrary URL or a catchphrase based short URL.
- wp.me: WordPress URL shortener
- Yep.it: Basic URL shortener

There are various administrations you can use to locate an accessible URL; however the most advantageous for finding a short URL is Domain. On the off chance that you compose in the word you need to incorporate into your short URL, this site will give the diverse ways you may amass it with an assortment of spaces. It additionally tells you which of these choices is accessible for procurement. Your URL should be less than 15 characters keeping in mind the end goal to work with Bitly.

Bit.ly:

In the event that you don't as of now have one, it is allowed to agree to accept a Bitly account. With the record, you'll have the capacity to set up your modified short URL and view insights on the altered short connections that you make. You'll have to check your email address before you can make a custom short area.

Sign into Bit.ly, and select 'Settings' starting from the full menu at the upper-right corner of the page. Tap on the 'Propelled' tab, and select either 'Individual' or 'Business' under the 'Custom Short Domain' header. Enter your short space; you'll need to set an A Record for your short area before you can confirm it (see underneath).

Sign into your area name enlistment center and set the A record, or DNS have, for your short URL to point to bit.ly's IP address (at Go Daddy, the A record is situated under the "DNS" tab in the Domain Manager). Bitly's IP address is 69.58.188.49. It can take up to 48 hours for area changes to produce results.

To track all the snap movement to your site, set up your following area under the 'Propelled' tab in your settings. Enter the area name you need to track (your site's long space) in your Bitly account. This area ought not to be the same as the short URL that you simply set up. After you check that you possess the URL (there are three approaches to give confirmation), Bitly will consequently change over any connections you abbreviate from that site to your custom short URL.

Offer Your Custom Links

When the majority of your virtual wires are associated, any URLs from your long area will be especially abbreviated, given that you are signed into your Bit.ly account. This set up won't modify connects to your site that others are sharing. That usefulness, as observed with The New York Times, is just accessible at an undertaking level Bit.ly organization. At the point when you achieve those 17 million unique for every month, let us know, and we'll demonstrate to you industry standards to kick it into high gear.

Make an abbreviated URL

1.   Visit the Google URL shortener site at goo.gl.
2.   If you aren't marked in, tap the Sign in catch in the upper right corner.
3.   Write or glue your URL in the Paste your long URL here box.
4.   Click Shorten URL.

Underneath the "Glue your URL here" box, you'll see the long form of your URL and the short form. Once made, your connection won't lapse unless it must be expelled for spam, protection, or lawful reasons.

Track the utilization of your URL

You can perceive what number of individuals has tapped on your URL by going to goo.gl.

For more definite data about the URL's utilization, including the nations, programs, and stages that got to it, include .information to the finish of your short URL. For instance, point by point following for http://goo.gl/l6MS can be found at http://goo.gl/l6MS.info.

Following for all goo.gl short connections are openly noticeable to all clients. Making joins when you're marked in versus marked out:

Marked in
- Your joins are naturally added to goo.gl where you can track their utilization.
- A one of a kind short URL is made each time a long URL is abbreviated.

Marked out
- Your joins won't appear on your goo.gl page.

- The same short URL is reused each time a long URL is abbreviated by you or another person.

Thoughts on how to utilize URL shorteners in your promoting:

1. Make interfaces more significant with a custom, short area

On the off chance that you ever happen to visit the Twitter channel for Mos., you may see something remarkable about their connections.

They're utilizing a custom short URL: mz.cm.
So connects this way:
https://moz.com/blog/declaring   mozcon-neighborhood 2016
http://mz.cm/1gpgLAJ

This can be an extremely incredible chance to broaden some marking into the abbreviated connections you share via web-based networking media. Furthermore, in any event, it could make for a fun examination to check whether it ups the commitment on your updates (I've heard a few people passage better with custom short URLs, some improve the situation with full URLs, and some improve the situation with buff.ly or bit.ly URLs.)

Kevin set up together this speedy video on the best way to set up a custom short space. You can purchase custom short spaces from destinations like Name.com and set them up to consequently abbreviate your connections with bit.ly and Buffer.

2. Track every one of the snaps perceives how things change after some time

Shortening joins is significant all by it—however, how would you know individuals are clicking them?

Uplifting news! Some URL shorteners let you track those connections, as well. There are a couple of ways these connections have a tendency to be followed:

Some URL shorteners track the connections themselves.
Bitly demonstrates to you how often one of your connections has been clicked, where the connection has been shared, and how other Bit.ly-abbreviated connections (Bit links) are directing people to a similar substance.

Some URL shorteners consequently connect Google Analytics following information.

Without a doubt, you can physically add UTM following codes to any connection, and afterward, abbreviate them down with a fundamental connection shortener. Be that as it may, a few instruments will let you preset those following codes and after that naturally annex them to whatever connections you abbreviate.

This is the place the Buffer connection shortener truly sparkles, as I would like to think. In case you're utilizing the Buffer for Business design, at that point, you can without much of a stretch (and consequently) add UTM following codes to any connection you share with Buffer. I'll demonstrate to you precisely best practices to do this later on

3. Alter an abbreviated bit.ly interface
One thing I adore about Bit.ly's connection shortening administration is the capacity to name short URLs. This implies we can turn a connection like this: http://bit.ly/1LYGfyq

Into something that mirrors the substance of the connection itself:
bit.ly/tips-4-tw (a connection to an article on twitter tips.

Modifying an abbreviated connection can be a fabulous method to give individuals a tad of setting for where they'll go when they click that small connection.

Add an abbreviated URL to your video

In case you're running an advertisement crusade that guides individuals to a specific site, you'll need individuals to recall where they should go. That can be precarious when you're managing a long, long URL. Yet, a connection shortener can make online goals significantly simpler to recollect.

For instance, I'm composing this article as Facebook dispatches its executioner new Lead Ads highlight. It's a sweet better approach to do focus on promoting. Be that as it may, all the sweet information about it is on a page with a truly long URL:

https://www.facebook.com/business/a/lead-promotions

A long URL like that won't be an issue—aside from that Facebook is instructing individuals about this new component through a video. Furthermore, I don't think about you, however, I'd have a harsh time recalling this URL in the wake of viewing a video.

Luckily for us, Facebook abbreviated that connect to a significantly more memory-accommodating

URL: fb.me/leads
That is considerably less demanding to recollect, and it looks super spotless toward the finish of this video.

Add an abbreviated URL to a plain-content email

A large portion of the connections individuals associate includes something other than a string of URL characters. We're all presumably used to clicking catches and message connections, and we don't frequently end up confronting a long URL head-on.

This can make experiencing long, "terrible" URLs (particularly ones all decked out with UTM codes) significantly all the more bumping for your group of onlookers, particularly in plain-content messages. Luckily, a short URL can turn a plain-content email with long, stringy URLs into a considerably more decipherable message.

Add an abbreviated URL to a print piece

Assume you needed to run a print promotion in a magazine for one of your items. You trust the promotion will direct people to your site, however, there's an issue: the perfect page you need to send individuals to be a long one.

Yet, in the event that you abbreviate that URL down, you may have something more paramount, as well as more printable, as well. You'll spare a greater amount of that important land for the genuine promotion content, and give less of it to attempting to make a long string of URL characters look beautiful.

How to Start Earning Using Short-Links:

All things considered, a large portion of us are of the feeling that profiting on the web is intense. Nonetheless, you will be happy to realize that there is a simple technique for acquiring cash on the web. Indeed, you can abbreviate URLs and profit. Today, we share with you 15 Best URL Shortener to Earn Money Online.

By utilizing URL Shortening Service or Website, you can gain cash online by shortening the long URLs from different sites. Best of all, you require not have any specialized abilities. In addition, it isn't required to have any blog or site. Nonetheless, in the event that you have one, it would be a reward for you.

The abbreviated URLs can be posted on your blog or site. You can likewise post the abbreviated URLs on discussions and also person to person communication stages, for example, Facebook, Twitter, Google+ or anyplace. At whatever point guest taps on your abbreviated URL, some cash will be credited to his/her URL Shortener Account. In this way, there is salary potential from each snap.

It is one of the least difficult techniques for procuring cash on the web. Nonetheless, now and again the URLs turn out to be long and monstrous. Also, once in a while the URLs can contain associate connections that individuals need to cover up. This caused interface sharing to drop down. With the approach of URL Shortener Services/Websites, everything turned out to be simple. You simply need to enter your long, terrible, or subsidiary connection in these URL Shortener Websites and they go ahead to make short and wonderful URL totally free. As time passed, URL Shortener Services wound up famous as they began paying individuals for shortening their URLs.

How URL Shortener Works

Unfailingly, when somebody taps on the abbreviated connection, you will get paid. These URL Shortener Services or Websites can pay as much as $4-$5 for every 1000 guests that you convey to your connection. They pay you as you convey activity to them. These guests will most likely turn into their new clients and clients

At the point when a guest taps on the given URL, the Shortened URL will sit tight for 5 seconds and afterward it will be diverted to the first goal interface. For these 5 seconds, URL Shortener administration will show an ad. As 5 seconds or all the more (contingent upon administration to benefit) is a finished page is diverted to the first goal.

It is prescribed to abstain from utilizing abbreviated URL on your site as it might disturb your guests superfluously. Ordinarily, you should utilize Shortened URL on discussions, and interpersonal interaction stages, for example, Facebook, Twitter, and Google+.

URL Shortener Image

The installment is made utilizing proper installment strategies that the sites are utilizing, for example, PayPal. Each URL Shortener Website or Service pays distinctive CPM rates. The CPM rate likewise relies upon the nation from where individuals are opening the abbreviated connections. Along these lines, the CPM rate you get relies upon the URL shortener organizations and in addition distinctive nations.

A decent URL Shortener site can pay to their distributor somewhere in the range of $1 to $10 per 1000 perspectives on the abbreviated URL. They likewise give a referral framework wherein in the event that anybody joins utilizing your referral connect then you will be qualified for getting up to 20% commission of their acquiring.

Instructions to Earn with URL Shortener

On the off chance that you need to win great sum with URL Shortener, at that point the most ideal path is to share another person post or article. Discover a portion of the famous destinations like news locales or viral news site. Utilize their URL and abbreviate that URL with URL shortener administrations and offer that article, news, drifting points, viral pictures, and recordings, and so on with your URL.

You can share those drifting point on your social profiles, gathering or social sharing destinations. Individuals adore perusing drifting news and will tap on your mutual URL, and you can profit with it.

- **Ouo.io**

Ouo.io is one of the quickest developing URL Shortener Service. Its lovely space name is useful in producing a bigger number of snaps than other URL Shortener Services, thus you get a decent open door for acquiring more cash out of your abbreviated connection. Ouo.io accompanies a few propelled includes and in addition customization choices.

With Ouo.io you can gain up to $8 per 1000 perspectives. It additionally tallies different perspectives from same IP or individual. With Ouo.io it turns out to be anything but difficult to gain cash utilizing its URL Shortener Service. The base payout is $5. Your profit is consequently credited to your PayPal or Payoneer account on first or fifteenth of the month.

- **Link shrink**

Link shrink URL Shortener Service gives you a chance to adapt joins that you go on the Internet. Link shrink comes as a standout amongst the most trusted URL Shortener Service. It gives a propelled detailing framework with the goal that you can without much of a stretch track the execution of your abbreviated connections. You can utilize Link shrink to abbreviate your long URL. With Link shrink, you can gain somewhere in the range of $3 to $10 per 1000 perspectives.

Link shrink gives bunches of customization alternatives. For instance, you can change URL or have some custom message other than the standard thing "Skirt this Ad" message for expanding your connection snaps and perspectives on the promotion. Link shrink additionally offers a level $25 commission on your referrals. The base payout with Link shrink is $5. It pays you through PayPal, Payza, or Bitcoin.

- **Negligible Link**

Abbreviate URLs and procure cash with Petty Link which is extraordinary compared to other URL Shortening for winning cash on the web.

The beginning is simple. You have to make a record, abbreviate your connection, and begin acquiring cash. Frivolous is a standout amongst other approaches to procuring additional cash.

You get the opportunity to profit from home while overseeing and securing your connection. Utilizing the Petty Link device, you can make short connections. What's ideal, you get paid. It's a totally free apparatus. You need to make a record, make a connection, and post it. For each visit, you gain cash. Also, you can get 21% Referral Bonus. It has the Petty Link Referral Program. Elude companions and get 21% of their profit forever.

Its highlighted Administration Panel enables you to control the majority of the highlights with a tick of a catch. It offers nitty-gritty details. You become more acquainted with your group of onlookers. It has a low least payout. You have to gain just $5.00 before you are paid. Installment strategy is PayPal. In addition, Petty offers the most noteworthy rates.

In addition, it has a devoted help group to enable you to out on the off chance that you have any inquiries or issues.

- **Shorte.st**

Shorte.st is another extremely prevalent and most trusted URL Shortening Company. Shorte.st comes as an easy to understand URL Shortener Service with numerous imaginative alternatives for profiting by adapting the connections you share. Shorte.it gives you a chance to procure from $5 to $15 per 1000 perspectives for advancing their abbreviated connections.

For WordPress Bloggers, Shorte.st brings its WordPress Plugin which will help you enormously to support your profit. Shorte.st has a low least payout of $5.

The installment is credited consequently on the tenth of every month. The installment strategies incorporate PayPal, Payoneer, and Web Money. It additionally exhibits a referral gaining opportunity wherein you can procure 20% commission on referrals for a lifetime.

- **Adf.ly**

Adf.ly is the most seasoned and a standout amongst the most trusted URL Shortener Service for profiting by contracting your connections. Adf.ly gives you a chance to procure up to $5 per 1000 perspectives. Be that as it may, the income relies on the socioeconomics of clients who go ahead to tap the abbreviated connection by Adf.ly.

It offers an extremely far-reaching detailing a framework for following the execution of your every abbreviated URL. The base payout is kept low, and it is $5. It pays on the tenth of consistently. You can get your income by means of PayPal, Payza, or Alert Pay. Adf.ly likewise runs a referral program wherein you can gain a level 20% commission for every referral for a lifetime.

- **Dwindle**

Dwindle is outstanding amongst other URL Shorten to acquire cash on the web. It offers the chance to win cash for each individual that perspectives join you have made. Its working is basic. You have to make a record and afterward abbreviate any URLs with a tick of a catch. Go ahead to share your abbreviated URLs on the web, including online networking, YouTube, web journals, and sites. Lastly, acquire when any individual taps on your abbreviated URL.

They offer the best condition to you for gaining cash from home. They have even thought of a referral framework where you can welcome individuals to Dwindle and win as much as 20% of their wage. It has worked in a special framework wherein you get the chance to expand your day to day benefits when you investigate your best movement sources and nitty-gritty details.

The best part is that you get the most astounding payout rates. The contents and the APIs enable you to win through your sites proficiently. Last however not the minimum you get installments on time inside four days.

- **Al.ly**

Al.ly is another extremely prevalent URL Shortening Service for acquiring cash on short connections without contributing any single $. Al.ly will pay from $1 to $10 per 1000 perspectives relying on the diverse locales. Least withdrawal is just $1, and it pays through PayPal, Payoneer, or Payza. In this way, you need to win just $1.00 to wind up qualified to get paid utilizing Al.ly URL Shortening Service.

Other than the short connections, Al.ly additionally runs a referral program wherein you can procure 20% commission on referrals for a lifetime. The referral program is a standout amongst other approaches to procuring much more cash with your short connections. Al.ly offers three diverse record memberships, including free choice and in addition to premium choices with cutting-edge highlights.

- **Link bucks**

Link bucks is another best and a standout amongst the most well-known locales for shortening URLs and acquiring cash. It gloats of high Google Page Rank and additionally high Alexa rankings. Link bucks is paying $0.5 to $7 per 1000 perspectives, and it relies upon the nation to nation.

The base payout is $10, and installment strategy is PayPal. It likewise gives the chance of referral profit wherein you can acquire 20% commission for a lifetime. Link bucks runs promoting programs too.

- **Fas.li**

In spite of the fact that Fas.li is generally new URL Shortener Service, it has made its name and is viewed as a standout amongst the most trusted URL Shortener Company. It gives a magnificent chance to acquiring cash online without spending even a solitary $. You can hope to gain up to $15 per 1000 perspectives through Fas.li.

You can begin by enlisting a free record on Fas.li, shrivel your imperative URLs, and offer it to your fans and companions in online journals, gatherings, web-based social networking, and so forth. The base payout is $5, and the installment is made through PayPal or Payza on first or fifteenth of every month.

Fas.li additionally runs a referral program wherein you can procure a level commission of 20% by alluding for a lifetime. Also, Fas.li isn't restricted in anyplace so you can procure from those spots where other URL Shortening Services are prohibited.

- **Short.am**

Short.am gives a major chance to acquiring cash by shortening joins. It is a quickly developing URL Shortening Service. You basically need to join and begin contracting joins. You can share the abbreviated connections over the web, on your page, Twitter, Facebook, and then some. Short.am gives nitty-gritty insights and simple to-utilize API.

It even gives additional items and modules with the goal that you can adapt your WordPress site. The base payout is $5 before you will be paid. It pays clients through PayPal or Payoneer. It has the best market payout rates, offering unparalleled income. Short.am additionally runs a referral program wherein you can acquire 20% additional commission forever.

- **Bc.VC**

Bc.vc is another awesome URL Shortener Site. It gives you a chance to gain $4 to $10 per 1000 visits on your Shortened URL. The base withdrawal is $10, and the installment strategy utilized by PayPal or Payoneer. Installments are made naturally on every seven days for income higher than $10.00. It additionally runs a referral framework wherein the rate of referral acquiring is 10%.

- **Urlcash.net**

Urlcash.net makes it extremely simple for you to acquire cash online by shortening URLs. It keeps running on the basic rationality of – influence it, to post it, and acquire it. Join is free. Urlcash offers day by day payout and installment is made by means of PayPal, Web Money, and Wire Transfer. You can profit by posting joins on your web journals, gatherings, sites, and web-based social networking sites. You get numerous highlights in Urlcash.

- **Usskip.me**

Uskip.me is a standout amongst the most dependable and reliable URL Shortener Service. It gives the chance to abbreviate the connections and gain cash. With Uskip.me, you can admire high rates, on-time installments, live details, and first-rate bolster. Best of all, Uskip.me has an overall nearness.

Installments are conveyed week after week and on-time. It pays by means of PayPal, Payza, Payoneer, and Web Money. Join is free and it takes barely one moment. It additionally runs a referral framework wherein you can procure 10% commission for alluding clients.

- **Space**

Space gives you a chance of acquiring cash online by sharing your connections, codes, glues utilizing its glue administrations. You can abbreviate and share joins whereby you can acquire up to $6 for every 1000 guests.

It offers one of the most astounding rates among contenders and other glue containers. The base payout is $5, and installment is made through PayPal. It additionally offers 5% referral reward.

- **Oke.io**

Oke.io gives you a chance to gain cash online by shortening URLs. Oke.io is an amicable URL Shortener Service as it empowers you to acquire cash by shortening and sharing URLs effortlessly.

Oke.io can pay you somewhere in the range of $5 to $10 for your US, UK, and Canada guests, though for whatever remains of the world the CPM won't be under $2. You can join by utilizing your email. The base payout is $5, and the installment is made by means of PayPal.

Step by step instructions to Shorten Links and Earn Money with Paid Link Shorteners. Did you realize that whenever you share your connection or connection to a bit of substance – you are leaving cash on the table in the event that you disregard this post since you could abbreviate interfaces and procure cash?

Paid connection shorteners are ignored by numerous however I will demonstrate to you how I utilize them to profit with my locales and put them all under a magnifying glass for the last time.

- What You Will Learn
- What interface shorteners are and for what reason to utilize them
- How paid shorteners function
- Step by step instructions to abbreviate interfaces and gain cash
- Which shortener is the most beneficial?
- What's more, how much cash you can make

Most sites profit through things like offering advertisement space, member items or their own particular computerized items et cetera. Some adaptation techniques are pretty much aloof, some require progressing work, some appear to suit a specific site well, others not really.

For those that don't have a clue about, a Link Shortener is a site or application that transforms long connections into short ones, that divert to the long connection

Here is a case of a long URL which focuses on the Amazon store:
http://www.amazon.com/Star-Wars-SignatureLightsaberRemovable/dp/B003I86C8U/ref=sr_1_1?s=toys-and-games&ie=UTF8&qid=1430138565&sr=1-1

Furthermore, here is its short form:
http://amzn.to/1OvdSOz

The short form just diverts you to the long form – which makes for less demanding sharing particularly on interpersonal organizations like Twitter. Utilizing a connection shortener is simple. Simply glue in the URL you need to abbreviate, click go and you are done.

It's just as simple as that!

Why Use A Link Shortener?
Spare space and "embellish" joins. Short connections look better and are easier to understand. For a few kinds of correspondences like instant messages or Twitter presenting it's critical on keep interfaces short to leave space for a message (as you presumably know a tweet is 140 characters in length)

Following, A few shorteners give insights about snaps, impressions and a scope of other trackable information. When you see an abbreviated URL, you don't know where you will arrive after you click it. Thus, a few people utilize this to mask the objective URL.

Lastly, Ladies and Gentlemen:
With this profiting method, you can acquire cash each time a short connection is clicked. Presently you have a general thought of how to connect shortener's function, how about we turn our consideration on the most proficient method to utilize them to profit! Not all shorteners let you win cash. So we will concentrate totally Paid Link Shorteners that give all of you the upsides of ordinary shorteners however with the additional capacity to profit.

How Paid Shorteners Work
On the off chance that you add a publicizing layer to a great shortener, you get paid connection shortener. The layer is included between an abbreviated URL and goal page and this is the means by which cash becomes an integral factor.

How it functions by and by:
Guest clicks an abbreviated connection (abbreviated URL)

The advertisement is shown on a middle page – you procure cash.

The guest is diverted from the middle page to the goal page (long URL)

This technique for winning cash makes them premium points of interest.

What I like most is that it doesn't devour land space of your sites that are better put to use for enhancing email transformation.

The most effective method to abbreviate connects and wins cash.

Also, you change leaving guests into a benefit and to wrap things up, short connections can be utilized all over, e.g. on Facebook pages, twitter, messages and so on.

Picking the Best Paid Link Shortener

When I found paid connection shorteners, they had all the earmarks of being an extraordinary extra stream of income for two of my sites, so I chose to try them out. The issue was I couldn't locate any believable data about the execution of the diverse organizations (there are a couple) and there were numerous opposite suppositions among clients. As I trust numbers and details more than feelings of easygoing clients, I chose to lead my own tests to locate the most elevated paying URL shortener that really pays out.

Presently I'm significantly more astute and I'd get a kick out of the chance to impart this information to you. I began with Google and did some exploration to get brands to test.

At last, I chose four brands:
Adf.ly
Shorte.st
Link Shrink
Ouo.io (choose to include this later, in the second test stage)

Adf.ly and Shorte.st appear to be the greatest players available: very great notoriety, nice payout rates, and quite a while in business.

Link Shrink and Ouo.io (how would they even articulate this name?!) are generally littler administrations and new in business contrasting with the other two.

I included them in the test on account of good payout rates and my interest in their execution as they battle with two in number players and need to procure themselves the greatest conceivable cut of this cake.

How I Collected and Analyzed Data
To investigate the execution of every shortener I gathered:

Extraordinary Clicks: what number one of a kind guest Link Clicks were created. This was the most essential data for me, as the execution of my sites (and most sites which utilize paid connection shorteners) base on special guests. I utilized Unique Clicks (guests) to figure eCPM. Income:

Connection Clicks: what number circumstances my presentation page was clicked.
The information originates from:
Connection Clicks and Unique Clicks I followed on my presentation page with Google Analytics. Income, Counted Views and Counted Visitors appears in Dashboard of every shortener.

Following Traffic with Google Analytics
I exploited Google Analytics occasion following accepted procedures to track the majority of my movement.

How I gather and estimated information (Analytics illustration)
This can be separated as Occasion Category (movement separated by the nation. E.g. most

limited/MX is a connection clicked by guests from Mexico). One of a kind Events (Unique Clicks)

Add up to Events (Link Clicks)
Information from Paid Shortener Dashboards
I made a couple of connections and sent them activity, one connection for each nation.
Realizing that, I could watch what numbers of perspectives were produced from every nation and relate this information with shorteners' details.

As I was already aware what number of Unique Visitors I'd sent to every shortener (my Google Analytics information) and how much cash I earned from this movement I could compute execution of every shortener.

Execution of every shortener is characterized by eCPM.
ECPM is figured by isolating aggregate profit by add up to a number of impressions in thousands.

Information Analysis: US Traffic on the principal day of testing, I chose to send movement to shorteners only from the US.

Information Analysis: Mixed Traffic Around then, for the following three days, I sent blended activity from various nations (counting the US). It would be ideal if you take note of that I included nations with to a great degree low rate so eCPM, at last, is much lower than we might want to see. Innovative site proprietors can join an assortment of strategies and utilize them all the while. You need to test a blend of methodologies to perceive what works best for you.

Be that as it may, today I will clarify another layer with paid connection shorteners and the consequences of my own tests – the shorteners that are the most productive. So read on in the event that you might want to include another incredible weapon of the decision to your site adaptation munitions stockpile!

Conclusion

There are two driving paid connection shorteners available: Shorte.st and Adf.ly.

Shorte.st performs marginally better with regards to profit and I didn't have any shocks like with Adf.ly (when my activity for the US halted to be adapted for no reason).

Other tried shorteners – Link Shrink and Ouo.io – are not all that great.

They assert high CPM rates, and as my test appeared, this isn't valid. All things considered, they changeover super terrible.

Wrapping It Up

Advertisements served by paid shorteners are not generally of high caliber and that is the motivation behind why they're not for everybody. Most site proprietors incline toward AdSense due to promotion quality and transformation.

Be that as it may, few out of every odd site can be acknowledged by Google and some of them are even prohibited sooner or later due to their substance.

So in the event that you battle with Google or your site is like the over ones, you may consider experimenting with a paid shortened and I trust that my benchmark will be helpful for you.